Loving The Wrong Person

By

Frances Pineri

Table of Contents

Loving the wrong Person

What makes us as human beings love the wrong person?

Why do we love the wrong person and keep loving them? *Is there even an answer? Or are there too many answers to count?* That's what I'm here to explore in this simple but powerful reflection on the mystery of love.

As we journey through life, we gather countless experiences, some good, some bad, and some... unforgettable. But love? Love is an experience that hits everyone differently. For some, it comes and goes, leaving faint marks. For others, it crashes in, shakes everything up, and leaves a permanent scar—or a treasure. And if you're one of the lucky ones, it might just happen once... and change everything.

Love can feel like a bouquet of roses, bright reds, cheerful yellows, unexpected oranges. It's full of life, beauty, and passion. It pulls you in, leaving you wanting more. But *how long does that feeling last?* Because here's the thing: love starts like magic—pure, innocent, and intoxicating. You learn about each other's quirks, laugh at each other's jokes, and maybe even dream of a future together.

Then... reality sets in. You see the good, the bad, and yes, even the ugly. And suddenly, you're faced with a choice: *Do I stay? Or do I go?*

By the time we get to that point, life might have thrown some unexpected curveballs. Maybe there's an unplanned pregnancy—*yeah, we're going there*—and suddenly, the stakes are higher. Some couples marry quickly "for the sake of the child." And while there's probably love or admiration between them (this isn't a one-night stand we're talking about... or is it?), it's not always the kind of love that lasts forever.

To my young ladies reading this... don't think it can't happen to you. Even one "just this once" moment can change your life in ways you never imagined.

But here you are. If you've ever experienced this kind of love, you know how real the struggles are. What started as a whirlwind romance has now turned into... well, a harsh reality. Co-parenting replaces passion. And the differences between you two? They're not just quirks or hormonal phases. They're foundational cracks—ones that no amount of "working on it" seems to fix.

Arguments become routine. Trust breaks down. *Infidelity creeps in— on one side, or maybe both.* And you start to wonder if your compatibility was just a fleeting illusion. But now there's more than just love at stake. Maybe there are kids involved, or a mortgage, shared bills, childcare expenses, and all the other responsibilities that keep your lives intertwined. You're no longer independent of each other—you're co-dependent.

Here's the truth: you may still *love* this person, but you're not *in love* with them anymore. So why stay? Is it for the kids? Because you do love them unconditionally, and leaving might turn their world upside down? Or is it because you've become so used to sharing responsibilities— splitting the bills, keeping the roof over your heads—that the thought of starting over feels impossible?

Deep down, though, you long for something else. For a love that makes your heart race again. And sometimes... it comes. It might be someone at work, someone in the same boat as you, or even someone completely unattached. Suddenly, the spark you thought had died forever is reignited. There's excitement, stolen moments, secret rendezvous.

And oh, the fire. The thrill. The kisses that take you *beyond the stars*. It's intoxicating—the kind of love you've always dreamed of, the kind you feel you *deserve* after all the heartache you've endured. But as time passes, even this new love isn't immune to reality.

What started as passion and romance becomes... complicated. Life creeps in: graduations, birthday parties, family vacations. The priorities of "home life" are still there, pulling your lover in another direction. And now, you feel the sting of being left behind. Jealousy sets in. Those once-magical stolen moments grow fewer and fewer. You go from being the center of someone's world to being... a secret.

Now what? Do you accept being the "other" forever—the mistress, the fling, the boy toy? Call it what you will. The affair might last weeks, months, even years. But as a single person in this situation, where does it leave you? Waiting. Always waiting. Cherishing stolen moments that are never enough. Wondering when—or if—you'll see each other again.

And then come the mind games. *Are they still into me? Why have the texts slowed down? Are they with someone else now?* The doubt is suffocating. Meanwhile, the married partner wrestles with their own guilt, knowing deep down you deserve more. More time, more attention, more love—*the kind they can't fully give you.*

So let's pause. Why do we, as human beings, love the wrong person? Is it wrong to have an affair with someone married? Or is it wrong for the married person to betray their spouse? And here's the big one: how wrong is it to stay in a relationship that no longer fulfills you—emotionally, sexually, or otherwise?

These aren't easy questions to answer. But maybe... *just maybe...* it's time to ask yourself: *What do I truly want? And what am I willing to risk to find it?*

Chapter 1:

The Work Environment

This is the number one place where love, heartbreak, and infidelity intertwine—right where emotions and workplace politics collide. Engaging in a relationship with a co-worker can be a labyrinth of complexities, for a multitude of reasons. These relationships often demand discretion, which can be an almost impossible feat when emotions are running high. The added element of being surrounded by colleagues, who may notice lingering glances or whispered conversations, can turn the once-private into public spectacle.

Jealousy can also rear its head in these situations, especially if one or both parties are charismatic or catch the eye of others. But, jealousy doesn't always have to be a negative force. In some cases, it can even fuel pride—a subtle reminder of your partner's appeal and the fact that, at the end of the day, they choose *you*. This perspective relies on the strength of the foundation you've built together. If that connection is solid, fleeting moments of admiration from others lose their power. However, if cracks already exist in that foundation, this attention can feel threatening, and insecurity can creep in.

Now, let's talk about the real risks here. Work relationships don't just challenge the emotional boundaries of a romance; they can also put your job, your reputation, and your professional credibility at risk. What starts as a passionate and exhilarating connection can spiral into awkwardness, stress, or even chaos if the relationship sours. Imagine the nightmare scenario of having to face an ex every single day at work—when avoidance isn't an option. Even worse, what if you discover you're not the only one involved, that there were other "relationships" happening in parallel? The tension and fallout from such revelations can be unbearable.

But let's shift the lens to a more hopeful picture for a moment. In some cases, workplace romances do blossom into something beautiful. Against all odds, these connections can lead to lasting love, shared lives, and a story that feels like a modern fairy tale. You meet, sparks fly, and somehow, it works. You make time for each other despite demanding schedules and separate responsibilities. A quick phone call to say "Good morning" or "Good night" becomes a lifeline. Even in the absence of physical presence, these small gestures reinforce the bond you're building.

It's easy to fall in love, but it's not always easy to know if you've fallen for the *right* person. When love is fresh, it's thrilling and full of potential, yet there's always a level of uncertainty. This is where the bedrock of any lasting relationship comes into play: honesty. Without honesty, there is no trust. Without trust, there is no stability. And without stability, there is no lasting connection.

Balance is crucial in any relationship. Both people need to be willing to compromise—not just on their beliefs or ideals, but on their time and priorities. A relationship asks you to give of yourself in ways that aren't always easy. Sometimes, you'll question your choices. You'll wonder, *What am I getting myself into? Is this worth it?* These questions are normal, even healthy, but they require you to dig deep and evaluate whether the love you've found is built on something real and enduring.

Love isn't always about grand gestures or idealized perfection. It's about patience, understanding, and the willingness to navigate life's uncertainties together. Relationships take work. They demand communication, a shared vision, and a commitment to weather the storms. Without these, the cracks will inevitably grow, and the foundation will crumble.

But if you're willing to put in the effort—if you can be honest with yourself and with your partner—then even in the face of challenges, there's hope. And sometimes, against all odds, it works out. Sometimes, you stay for the long haul and find that the love you've built is worth every trial along the way.

Chapter 2:

The Relationship Begins

Here we are in what feels like an established relationship—or is it? *What do we even call this?* To the two people involved, it feels real. You're spending time together, sharing intimate moments, laughing, and maybe even leaning on each other during tough times. But for some reason, it's all kept quiet. Maybe it's because of outside circumstances, fear of judgment, or just the simplicity of keeping things private. Whatever the reason, the connection grows.

Over time, it becomes more than just physical or casual. Your partner starts to feel like your rock—the one who listens when your day has been a mess, the one who reassures you when life gets overwhelming. They're there for you in ways you didn't expect, and you find yourself opening up to them. *This person knows the parts of you that you don't share with anyone else.*

You share laughter, your fears, even your dreams. It feels natural. You meet each other's families or friends, and even those around you begin to notice how often you're together. Whether it's a weekly meet-up or just the occasional moment stolen from a busy life, you build a rhythm that feels steady. The relationship takes root.

But no relationship is without its challenges. There are disagreements. Sometimes arguments. You compromise, talk things through, and eventually move forward. Every resolution feels like a step toward something stronger, something more lasting. You start to feel comfortable in this partnership, knowing you can count on each other.

And let's be honest—it feels good. Having someone to listen to you, to support you, to satisfy your needs emotionally and physically... *it feels like everything is falling into place.*

But here's where things can take a turn. Without realizing it, those little things you once appreciated start to feel... routine. You forget to acknowledge them. One person may begin to give more, while the other takes more. It's rarely intentional—it's just how life happens sometimes. But slowly, the balance shifts.

When that balance tilts too far, cracks start to show. The person giving more begins to feel weighed down—not just by their own struggles, but by carrying the emotional load for both people. And maybe they don't say anything, because *who wants to feel like a burden?* But that weight can quietly start to break them.

This is the moment that defines the future of the relationship. Do you both recognize the imbalance and work to fix it? Or do you let it go unspoken, allowing resentment to quietly grow? Because here's the truth: once someone feels unheard, unappreciated, or overburdened, the foundation you've built begins to crumble.

The real test isn't the good times. It's the hard moments. It's the willingness to sit down and say, *"This isn't working for me—how do we fix it together?"* It's the decision to keep trying, even when things feel messy, because you remember why you started in the first place.

But if that effort isn't mutual... if one person keeps carrying the weight alone... even the strongest relationship can fall apart. *And that's when you have to ask yourself: is this what I want? Is this enough?*

Because love, at its core, isn't just about being there for someone— it's about being there for each other.

Chapter 3:

The Strain

The relationship starts to strain when communication begins to break down. At first, it might seem minor—maybe one person feels unheard or dismissed during conversations. Or maybe the other just doesn't see the point of talking anymore, feeling like it's not worth the effort. *But here's the thing about communication—it's the glue that holds everything together.* When it falters, wedges begin to form, creating space that grows wider with every unresolved issue.

Soon, there's less talking and more tension. Arguments become frequent. The fights get uglier. Name-calling, finger-pointing, and accusations fill the silence that once held laughter and connection. The emotional baggage starts piling up, and suddenly, the relationship feels more like a weight than a comfort. Time together begins to feel irrelevant—like it could be better spent somewhere else, with someone else, or even alone in peace.

And here comes the breaking point. *What happens next determines everything.* Do you both recognize what's happening and try to bridge the gap, or do you let the cracks grow until the relationship falls apart?

As people, we're drawn to the things that connect us—shared values, dreams, and goals. But even with those connections, one undeniable truth remains: *without chemistry, without attraction, no amount of effort will make it work.* You can try to hold on, but eventually, you'll find that the ends never meet. And when a relationship starts to crumble, the strain doesn't just stay between the two people involved. If children are part of the equation, the challenges multiply.

Take holidays, for instance. What should be joyful occasions can become nightmares of logistics and divided loyalties. Who gets the kids this year? Who celebrates on the actual holiday, and who has to settle for the day after? The emotional weight of making those decisions—while trying to hide the stress from the children—can be overwhelming.

It gets even more complicated if there's another person involved—someone outside the official relationship. For those in secret or hidden romances, holidays can be some of the most isolating times. While the "official" family celebrates together, the other person is left on the sidelines, waiting, knowing they'll only get scraps of time—if any. *And let's be real, this kind of dynamic doesn't just hurt; it eats away at the heart of any connection.*

The truth is, situations like these force you to confront the reality of your choices. Maybe, just maybe, you're with the wrong person. What once felt meaningful and full of potential has been interrupted by harsh realities—unspoken doubts, unmet needs, and the undeniable sense that something's missing.

It's a painful realization, but one that many face: *Loving the wrong person can feel like a prison you never meant to walk into.* And the longer you stay, the harder it becomes to see a way out.

Chapter 4:

Fight or Flight

Do you stay or go? Does any of it even make sense anymore? You sit there, lost in your thoughts, going over the same questions again and again. *How did we get here? Was it something I said?* You replay conversations in your mind, overanalyzing every word. Where once you felt free and confident, now you're walking on eggshells. It feels like everything you say is picked apart, judged, or dismissed. The connection that once felt so natural now feels like a fragile thread that might snap at any moment.

And so, time becomes crucial. Do you fight for this relationship, for what you believed was real? Or do you give it space and hope that things fix themselves? *Spoiler alert: they don't.* Space, more often than not, creates distance—not just physical, but emotional. It lets doubt creep in, telling one or both of you that maybe it's easier to be alone than to keep trying to fix something that feels broken.

But then there's the flip side. After all the time, energy, and love you've invested, *shouldn't it be worth the fight?* Many people would argue, "Yes, absolutely!" Emotions run high, and before you know it, a battle begins—not just with your partner, but within yourself. You're caught between wanting to hold on and feeling like you're grasping at something that's already slipping away.

And what happens when the fight consumes you? When your thoughts are no longer about the joy you once shared but about the endless struggle to bring it back? Now, it feels like you're living separate lives—on opposite sides of a street, walking in different directions. The connection fades, replaced by distractions. New people, new conversations, new places suddenly catch your attention. You spend less time together, more time apart. Excuses come easily—working late, catching up with old friends. *But deep down, you know what's happening.*

No matter how strong you think you are, there's always something—or someone—that can test you. Maybe it's someone who makes you laugh again. Someone who sees you in a way that feels refreshing, exciting, even dangerous. Choices are decisions we all face, whether we like it or not. And these moments of temptation or clarity force us to confront the truth: *Is this relationship worth saving? Or has it run its course?*

And then there's the family. Meeting them can feel like stepping into a courtroom. Judgment, suspicion, and silent stares greet you before a word is even spoken. They dissect everything—how you talk, how you walk, how you drink your coffee. Maybe they don't like the way you laugh. Maybe they think you're too much, or not enough. And if the relationship is already shaky, this added layer of scrutiny can feel like the final nail in the coffin. *Is this really where I belong? Did I fall for the wrong person?*

The hardest decision of all lies in that quiet moment when you ask yourself, *Do I stay, or do I go?* Love can make fools of us, no doubt about it. It can blind us, pull us into situations we never imagined, and keep us there long after the spark has faded.

But then there's the other side of love—the part that goes beyond passion and physical attraction. The part that makes you value the time and energy you've poured into this person, into this relationship. *What if this is as good as it gets?* You start to weigh the pros and cons, replaying the good moments, the bad moments, and the moments that left you questioning everything.

The scales tip back and forth. One moment, you're convinced it's over; the next, you're clinging to hope. Because as much as love can hurt, it's also rare. It's not something you can count on finding again. And so, you sit with the same question circling in your mind: *Do I stay and fight, or do I let go and move on?*

Only you can decide. And that's the hardest part of all.

Chapter 5:

Guidance

Now begins the journey of one last attempt to salvage what's left of this relationship. You find yourself reaching out for guidance—any kind you can get. You talk to friends, family members, or even a stranger who happens to strike up a conversation at just the right time. *Maybe they're going through something too, and misery loves company.* For some, the search for answers leads to a counselor or therapist. Others turn to horoscopes or spiritual readings, trying to prepare themselves for the unknown, clinging to the hope that the stars will point them in the right direction.

As you seek advice, you notice a pattern. You make excuses for their bad behavior—convincing yourself it's not as bad as it seems. But then there's the hard part: facing your own role in the relationship. *No one likes admitting they're wrong, especially when it's a pattern they've repeated over and over.* The truth stings, but it's there—waiting for you to confront it.

After countless conversations with friends and family, you eventually arrive at a decision. You tell yourself to stick with what you know. Why? Because starting over is terrifying. The idea of jumping into the unknown—risking the possibility of ending up in an even worse situation—feels overwhelming. For some, it's not just fear but practicality. *It's cheaper to keep them.* The thought of paying child support, dividing assets, or walking away from the life you've worked so hard to build is enough to keep you holding on, even if it means sacrificing your happiness.

And then there's the classic saying: *The grass isn't always greener on the other side.* What if leaving doesn't solve anything? What if you're just trading one set of problems for another? As these thoughts circle in your mind, you realize something important—it doesn't really matter what advice anyone gives you. At the end of the day, people follow their hearts, no matter how irrational it may seem. *We love what we know—even if it's not good for us.*

When the decision is made without emotion—when it's purely logical—the outcome feels cold and distant. If you choose to stay, it's not out of love but out of convenience. You live separate emotional lives while sharing the same physical space. The relationship becomes a co-existence, a quiet agreement that you'll each do as you please with no expectations of reconciliation. It's a life of going through the motions, but with no real connection.

On the other hand, if the decision is to leave, that's when the real fight begins. Who gets what? How will custody be divided if there are children? The once-shared dreams of building a life together become nothing more than a list of items to be split: the house, the car, the bank accounts. What once felt like a partnership becomes a battle, with lawyers, court dates, and arguments over who deserves what.

And through it all, you're left wondering... *Was it worth it? Should I have stayed and found a way to make it work?* But deep down, you already know the answer. Whether you stay or go, the real question isn't about what's easier or more practical—it's about what will bring you peace. Because at the end of the day, peace is what we're all searching for, even if it means walking away from everything you thought you'd never lose.

Chapter 6:

When the Love is Gone

When all is said and done, and the love you once felt has faded into something unrecognizable, you're left with a heavy question: *Can I face life alone?* The idea of starting over by yourself can feel overwhelming. How do you even begin to untangle the life you've built together when your partner has become all you know? You might no longer feel respect or affection for them, but the thought of moving on still feels impossible.

Then there's the bigger picture to consider. *What happens to the children?* If you have kids together, you start to wonder how your decision will affect them. How do you handle it when your children seem to have a better relationship with your partner than you do? When they talk to your partner with ease, but your own conversations are reduced to silence or surface-level exchanges? And what about the realization that your partner isn't coming home for *you* anymore, but for the comfort of the house, the kids, or even the family pet? It's a crushing feeling to recognize that your presence no longer seems to matter in the place you call home.

And then there's betrayal. Betrayal can take so many forms— cheating, verbal abuse, mental manipulation, even physical violence. Whatever form it takes, betrayal cuts deeper than almost anything else. For the person on the receiving end, it can leave scars that don't just heal with time. *It hurts in ways you can't put into words.* The physical and emotional toll can be overwhelming. Some people stop eating, lose weight, or fall into depression. The betrayal can haunt their thoughts, making it hard to focus on daily life or even imagine trusting someone again.

The worst part of betrayal isn't just the pain—it's the way it makes you doubt everything. You start to question the past, the relationship, and yourself. It can leave you feeling broken, angry, inadequate, or simply numb. And when you're in that place, it's hard to believe that love—real, healthy, genuine love—could ever find you again. *But here's the truth:*

betrayal doesn't define your worth, and it doesn't mean you won't find love again.

For the person doing the betraying, guilt often becomes its own poison. They might lash out, become argumentative, or try to shift blame to avoid confronting their own actions. They know they're hurting the relationship, but instead of facing the guilt, they create even more chaos. And the person on the receiving end is left trying to make sense of it all. *Why is this happening? What did I do wrong?* You give them the benefit of the doubt, because who wants to believe their partner could hurt them like this? You think, *Maybe they're just stressed. Maybe I should give them space. Maybe I should bend a little more to keep the peace.* But deep down, you know the truth: none of these "maybes" will fix the pain you're feeling.

The emotions that follow betrayal are never positive. They're heavy, suffocating, and relentless. No one deserves to live in a relationship where negativity has taken over—where there's no trust, no respect, and no real love left to hold on to.

Here's the thing: *everyone deserves better.* You deserve real love. A connection that feels genuine, uplifting, and safe. A relationship where you're valued, respected, and cherished. Love isn't meant to tear you down or make you feel small—it's meant to help you grow, to carry you through the hard times, to celebrate the good times, and to hold you steady when life feels uncertain.

It's hard to walk away from something that you've put so much time and effort into. It's hard to let go of what's familiar, even when it's no longer healthy. But staying in a relationship where betrayal, neglect, or indifference have taken over isn't the answer. Real love is out there. And most often, it finds you when you least expect it.

So, be patient with yourself. Heal. Take the time to remember your worth, because *you are worthy of love.* The kind of love that doesn't just survive—but thrives. The kind of love that fills your soul, not drains it. It's waiting for you. You just have to be ready to let it in.

Chapter 7:

Healing

Healing begins when you finally accept the truth: *You loved the wrong person.* It's not an easy truth to face, but it's the first step toward freedom. It's about letting go of the life you thought you'd have with them and embracing the possibility of something better—a life where you can rediscover who you are, find your own happiness, and open your heart to love again. It's choosing not to let the pain of the past hold you hostage, refusing to let those bad experiences block the path to your future joy.

Healing means taking a chance—a leap of faith—to fill your life with purpose and meaning. It's about surrounding yourself with people who value and respect you, and in turn, giving that respect back. It's building relationships based on mutual care, not manipulation or control. And most importantly, it's reclaiming the parts of yourself that were lost in the chaos.

One of the most empowering realizations is this: *You didn't lose the love of your life. You lost a parasite.* You lost someone who drained your energy, stole your peace, and prevented you from living a fulfilling life. Toward the end, you may have come to dislike the person they showed themselves to be—but that's who they always were. When you see this clearly, the blame you've been placing on yourself begins to dissolve.

Yes, every action causes a reaction—that's undeniable. But healing isn't about playing the blame game. *Who started what doesn't matter anymore.* What matters is this: neither of you could reconcile the differences or find a way to compromise. And while that hurts, it's also freeing. It gives you the clarity to move forward, to stop carrying the weight of someone else's mistakes as if they're your own.

Breaking free from a toxic relationship takes an incredible amount of courage, strength, and resilience. It's not easy to walk away from something you've invested so much of your time and heart into, even when it's no longer healthy. But when the relationship has become a cycle of false promises, fake emotions, and toxicity, walking away isn't just an option—it's a necessity.

True healing comes when you can sit with yourself, alone, and not feel lonely. When you realize that everything you've been through didn't break you—it built you. It gave you strength, dignity, and the determination to never let yourself fall into the same traps again. *It's not about being perfect; it's about being wiser.* You've gained the experience to recognize red flags, to protect your heart, and to seek out genuine connections.

Of course, as humans, we are bound to make mistakes—we're imperfect by nature. But every mistake brings a lesson, and every lesson brings growth. Healing isn't about never falling again; it's about knowing how to pick yourself up when you do.

And then, there's the ultimate test of letting go. When you or your partner can walk away without looking back—after all attempts to reconcile have failed—you know it's time to move on. Whether you waited outside their home or workplace, sent countless texts, left messages that went unanswered, or tried every possible way to reach them, the silence speaks louder than words. *That's when you know: you loved the wrong person.*

But here's the beauty in all of this—healing is not the end of the story. It's the beginning of a new chapter. One where you are stronger, wiser, and open to the possibility of finding the love you truly deserve. Because love is out there. And this time, you'll know what real love looks and feels like when it finds you.

Written by Frances Ramos

www.ingramcontent.com/pod-product-compliance
Lightning Source LLC
Chambersburg PA
CBHW070959120626
46546CB00004B/1687